POSITIONS IN
LACROSSE

EMMETT MARTIN

PowerKiDS
press

New York

T0026816

Published in 2023 by The Rosen Publishing Group, Inc.
29 East 21st Street, New York, NY 10010

Portions of this work were originally authored by Ryan Nagelhout and published as *Lacrosse: Who Does What?* All new material in this edition was authored by Emmett Martin.

Editor: Therese Shea
Book Design: Michael Flynn

Photo Credits: Cover (lacrosse ball) Crucible Pictures/Shutterstock.com; (series jersey texture) Lemonsoup14/Shutterstock.com; cover (grass texture) comzeal images/Shutterstock.com; cover (lacrosse play) Dejan Popovic/Shutterstock.com; p. 5 (main) https://commons.wikimedia.org/wiki/File:George_Catlin_-_Ball-play_of_the_Choctaw-Ball_Up_-_Google_Art_Project.jpg; pp. 5 (inset), 9 (inset) Brian McEntire/Shutterstock.com; p. 6 https://commons.wikimedia.org/wiki/File:HSBC_Arena_Lacrosse.jpg; p. 7 Vladimir Korostyshevskiy/Shutterstock.com; p. 9 Mike Orlov/Shutterstock.com; p. 11 jaboardm/iStock; pp. 13, 19 enterlinedesign/Shutterstock.com; p. 14 JoeSAPhotos/Shutterstock.com; pp. 15, 27 James A Boardman/Shutterstock.com; p. 17 Marcelo Murillo/Shutterstock.com; pp. 21 (both), 23 James A Boardman/Shutterstock.com; p. 25 Rich Barnes/CSM via ZUMA Wire/AP Images; p. 26 aabejon/Shutterstock.com; p. 29 vernonwiley/iStock.

Library of Congress Cataloging-in-Publication Data

Names: Martin, Emmett, author.
Title: Positions in lacrosse / Emmett Martin.
Description: New York : PowerKids Press, [2023] | Series: Positions on the
  Team | Includes index.
Identifiers: LCCN 2022002727 (print) | LCCN 2022002728 (ebook) | ISBN
  9781538387115 (Library Binding) | ISBN 9781538387092 (Paperback) | ISBN
  9781538387108 (Set) | ISBN 9781538387122 (eBook)
Subjects: LCSH: Lacrosse–Juvenile literature.
Classification: LCC GV989.14 .M27 2023 (print) | LCC GV989.14 (ebook) |
  DDC 796.36/2–dc23/eng/20220215
LC record available at https://lccn.loc.gov/2022002727
LC ebook record available at https://lccn.loc.gov/2022002728

Manufactured in the United States of America

Some of the images in this book illustrate individuals who are models. The depictions do not imply actual situations or events.

CPSIA Compliance Information: Batch #CSPK23. For Further Information contact Rosen Publishing, New York, New York at 1-800-237-9932.

Find us on

CONTENTS

A SPORT WITH HISTORY

Sports are a passion of people around the world. The sport of lacrosse is beloved for a special reason: its extraordinary history. Native Americans were playing a lacrosse-like game before Europeans arrived in North America. It was different than what you might picture. Haudenosaunee (or Iroquois) peoples played games with over 1,000 participants! Over the years, the sport we know today as lacrosse emerged.

There's much to learn about modern lacrosse, and the rules and positions depend on the kind and league of lacrosse. The aim remains the same: your team needs to score more goals than the opponents.

ALL IN THE NAME

Early French settlers in Canada saw native peoples playing a game with sticks and a ball. They thought the sticks looked like the staff, or crosier, that their church bishops carried, which they called *la crosse*. That name stuck for Europeans. Today, a lacrosse stick is often called a crosse.

Some Native Americans called their lacrosse game *baggataway* or *tewaraathon*. The Cherokee described their game as the "little brother of war."

WHICH KIND OF LACROSSE?

It might surprise you to learn that men's and women's lacrosse have different rules. The key difference is that women's lacrosse is a noncontact sport, which means the players aren't supposed to touch each other's bodies.

BOX LACROSSE

Box lacrosse is a form of the sport played in a smaller area than field lacrosse. Box lacrosse is often played on a surface called the floor or carpet, which is about the size of a hockey rink. Some teams play on a turf-covered hockey rink. There are only six players on the floor for each box lacrosse team.

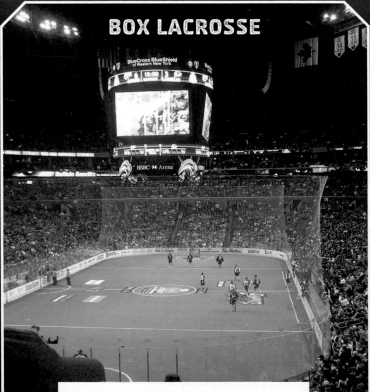

BOX LACROSSE

The National Lacrosse League (NLL) is a men's professional box lacrosse league in North America.

Other big differences between the two games are the numbers of players on the field and the size of the fields. In men's lacrosse, 10 people play on each team, and the two nets are 80 yards (73 m) apart. In women's lacrosse, 12 players from each team score on nets 90 to 100 yards (82 to 91 m) apart. The field itself in women's lacrosse is often longer too.

THINK FAST!

IN **NCAA** AND PRO MEN'S LACROSSE, A GAME IS USUALLY FOUR 15-MINUTE QUARTERS. IN 2021, THE NCAA DECIDED WOMEN'S LACROSSE WOULD SWITCH FROM 30-MINUTE HALVES TO 15-MINUTE QUARTERS.

FIELD LACROSSE

GET THE GEAR

Men's and women's lacrosse use slightly different lacrosse equipment. Women's field lacrosse sticks are shorter, for example, and players don't have to wear helmets if they don't play goalie. They do need to wear eye protection and a mouth guard. Some wear special gloves too.

Men's lacrosse allows body contact, so players need to wear more pads, including shoulder pads, arm pads, and gloves. They also need a helmet and mouth guard to keep them safe.

Goalkeepers in both sports wear extra equipment because they have to stop high-speed lacrosse balls. This includes a helmet with a face mask, a chest protector, and a throat protector.

STICK TO IT

Lacrosse sticks are different in men's and women's leagues. A men's lacrosse stick has a deep net used to cradle, or carry, a ball. A stick for women's lacrosse has a smaller net that's more for moving or passing the ball. Officials may inspect the sticks to make sure they're permitted.

THINK FAST!

LACROSSE STICKS CAN BE DIFFERENT SIZES DEPENDING ON A PLAYER'S POSITION. DEFENDERS HAVE LONGER STICKS THAN ATTACKERS.

You can see how men's and women's lacrosse differs in the equipment they use.

THE GOALIE

Men's lacrosse has four basic positions: goalkeepers, defenders, midfielders, and attackers. The most familiar is probably the goalkeeper (or goaltender). More commonly called the goalie, this player defends the net by standing in the crease, which is the circular area that surrounds the goal. The goalie needs to have quick **reflexes** to get in front of hard shots by the other team's offense. Goalies need to watch the action and follow the ball, down the field or behind the net.

Goalies have a special lacrosse stick with a much bigger net than other players'. They wear special gloves to protect their hand and especially thumbs.

TALK IT OUT

Goalies need to talk to their team when they see what's happening. A goalie can help their defenders stay in front of the other team's attack and make sure opponents don't get open for free shots. They can also start their team's offense with a good pass if they block a shot and get possession of the ball.

GOALIES ARE THE ONLY ONES ON THE FIELD WHO CAN TOUCH THE BALL WITH THEIR HANDS, BUT ONLY IN THE CREASE. THEN, THEY HAVE FOUR SECONDS TO PASS OR RUN WITH THE BALL, OR THEIR TEAM LOSES POSSESSION.

A goalie needs pads and a helmet like this to stop tough shots!

THE DEFENDERS

The players in men's lacrosse who are in charge of stopping their opponent's offense are called the defenders (or defensemen). The three defenders need to have fast feet to keep up with the offensive players called attackers. They know how to slide over to get in front of attackers who are passed the ball. Getting in their way can stop easy shots on net and help out their goalie.

Defenders also need to watch for players without the ball who are cutting toward the net looking for passes. Defenders' longer sticks help them block and even reach in to **intercept** passes and shots.

DEFENDING THEIR END

Generally, defenders stay in the defensive area during play. Even if the ball goes to a team's offensive end, the three defenders don't follow their teammates onto that side of the field. They have to stay back and watch what happens. They make sure they're ready for play to come back, though!

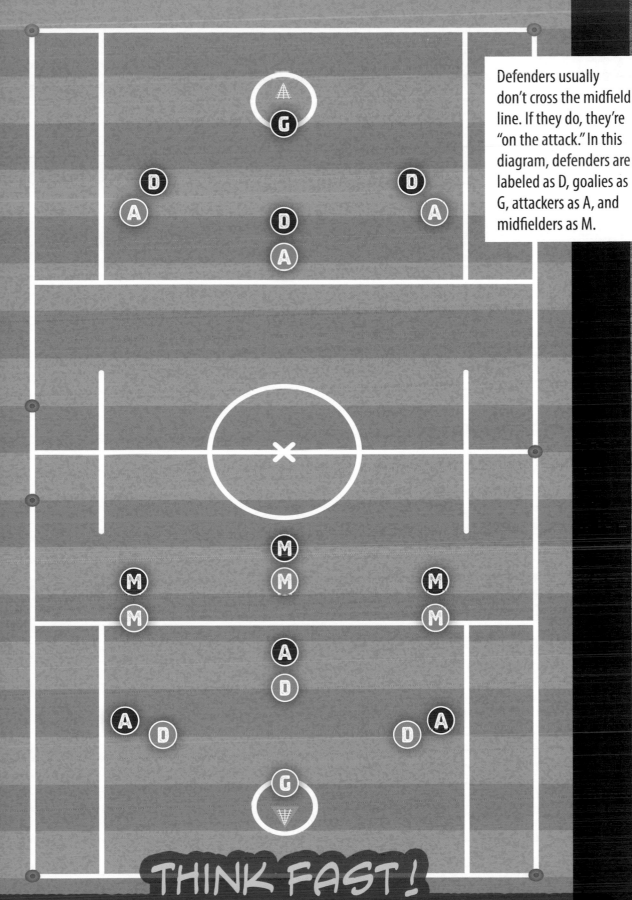

Defenders usually don't cross the midfield line. If they do, they're "on the attack." In this diagram, defenders are labeled as D, goalies as G, attackers as A, and midfielders as M.

THINK FAST!

DEFENSIVE PLAYERS CAN LEAVE THEIR END AS LONG AS ANOTHER TEAMMATE STAYS BEHIND TO KEEP THE NUMBER OF DEFENDERS IN THAT END AT FOUR. IF THERE ARE FEWER THAN FOUR DEFENDERS IN THE DEFENSIVE END, HOWEVER, POSSESSION IS GIVEN TO THE OPPONENT.

THE MIDFIELDERS

Midfielders play both offense and defense on a men's lacrosse team. These three players can move all over the field, helping the defense stop the other team from scoring and setting up attackers with good passes. While midfielders don't score very often, they can take shots on net and need to be smart to know where to be on the field at all times.

READING THE PLAY

Reading a play, or seeing where the ball is going and what the other team is doing, is a big part of a midfielder's job. Making a long pass to an attacker when the opponent's midfielders are out of position can lead to a chance for their team to score!

Midfielders help a team transition, or move from defense to offense and back again, without getting called **offside**. A great midfielder helps on both sides of the game, playing tough defense and helping teammates score in a matter of seconds!

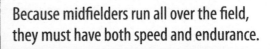

THINK FAST!
MIDFIELDERS ARE SOMETIMES CALLED "MIDDIES" FOR SHORT.

Because midfielders run all over the field, they must have both speed and endurance.

THE ATTACKERS

Attackers are on the field to score. The three attackers on a men's lacrosse team stay on the attacking side of the field. These players are fast and can shoot with great **accuracy**. They use shorter sticks, which make it easier to catch and throw. They must be able to get into scoring position and catch a pass from the midfielders while the other team's defenders buzz around them.

Getting away from the other team's defenders is important in lacrosse. Attacking players often cross paths with each other to mix up defenders and get open for scoring chances. This is called setting a pick.

OUT OF BOUNDS

In field lacrosse, the ball often goes out of bounds. If the ball leaves play after a shot, the team that has a player closest to the ball is given possession. If the ball leaves play for another reason, like a player running out of bounds with it, the team that didn't touch it last is given possession.

THINK FAST!

ATTACKERS MUST BE TOUGH TO MAINTAIN POSSESSION OF THE BALL AFTER GETTING **BODY CHECKED** BY A DEFENDER! THEIR SHORTER STICKS HELP THEM PROTECT THE BALL FROM STICK CHECKS.

Attackers need to have great stick-handling skills to protect the ball from defenders.

LEARN ABOUT WOMEN'S LACROSSE

Because women's lacrosse doesn't allow contact, the game focuses on speed and **agility**. Women's lacrosse has the same four basic positions as men's lacrosse but has two more players on each team. Each player's role is slightly different.

Women's lacrosse shares an offside rule with men's lacrosse. In women's lacrosse, seven field players can cross into the offensive side of the restraining line and four (plus the goalie) must stay behind. This limits the amount of attackers in the offensive zone. An extra player crossing the restraining line is offside and a foul is called, giving the other team a chance at scoring.

LEARNING THE LINES

Rather than one line at midfield as in men's lacrosse, women's lacrosse has restraining lines 30 yards (27 m) from each goal. This limits the number of offensive and defensive players around the ball at one time. Around each goal are two semicircle lines that are used to place players after a foul is called.

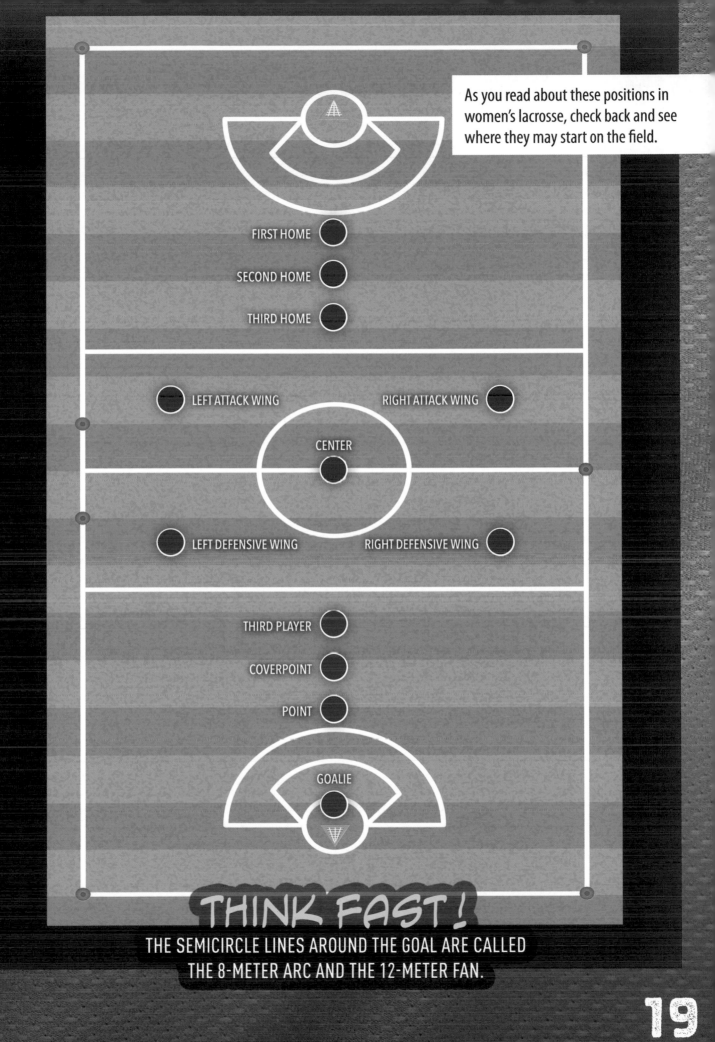

As you read about these positions in women's lacrosse, check back and see where they may start on the field.

FIRST HOME

SECOND HOME

THIRD HOME

LEFT ATTACK WING

RIGHT ATTACK WING

CENTER

LEFT DEFENSIVE WING

RIGHT DEFENSIVE WING

THIRD PLAYER

COVERPOINT

POINT

GOALIE

THINK FAST!
THE SEMICIRCLE LINES AROUND THE GOAL ARE CALLED
THE 8-METER ARC AND THE 12-METER FAN.

ON POINT

In women's lacrosse, the point is the defender guarding the first home, the name for the attacker closest to the net. The point works with the goalie to organize the defense. Points tell their fellow defenders where to go on the field. The point should be able to stick check and intercept passes.

Coverpoint is another important defensive position. Coverpoints need good footwork to stay with the offensive player called the second home, who's known as a playmaker for the offense. The coverpoint also takes passes from the goalie and looks for teammates up the field who can receive the ball.

THE THIRD PLAYER'S ROLE

The third player (or third man) is another defensive position. The third player's job is to cover the opponent's offensive player called the third home, who brings the ball from defense to attack. The third player needs to have good reflexes to keep track of this speedy opponent. Third players read the other team's offense to plug up passing lanes and break up plays.

THINK FAST!

IN WOMEN'S LACROSSE, LIKE IN MEN'S, A PLAYER CAN HIT AN OPPONENT'S STICK WITH THEIR OWN TO MAKE THE BALL COME OUT OF THE STICK'S NET. THIS IS CALLED A STICK CHECK.

Defenders in women's lacrosse play certain roles to stop opponents' attackers from scoring.

IN THE MIDDLE

The midfielder called the center is often found in the middle of the field in women's lacrosse. Centers take draws, sometimes called face-offs, and play both defense and offense. Centers are among their team's best players. They play all over the field and have many skills that make them good at attacking or defending.

The left and right defensive wings, or defense wings, start on the sides of the center circle, near the sidelines. These players guard the attack wings of the other team. Defensive wings often carry the ball into the attack area for their own team.

WIN THE DRAW!

A draw—or face-off—is the way that play starts or restarts in lacrosse. The centers in women's lacrosse put their sticks together, and an official puts the ball between the sticks. When the whistle blows, the players **maneuver** their sticks to get possession of the ball. In men's lacrosse, two players fight for a ball on the ground between them.

THINK FAST!

LACROSSE FANS KNOW THAT CONTROLLING DRAWS MEANS CONTROLLING THE GAME. CENTERS PRACTICE DIFFERENT METHODS TO WIN THE DRAW.

In women's lacrosse, a draw (also called a face-off) starts play at the beginning of both halves as well as after every goal.

ADDING TO THE ATTACK

Of the three main attack positions in women's lacrosse, the third home is often the best passer. Third homes set up the offense by feeding passes to the second and first home players, who are often in better positions to score. A third home sometimes takes shots on net but is usually best at getting assists.

The left and right attack wings transition the ball from defense to offense. Wings play on the outside edges of the field and help the home players score goals. They may not score many goals themselves, but are often responsible for helping make them happen.

PENALTIES

When a team breaks certain rules in lacrosse, such as pushing and holding, they may be called for a foul. The **penalty** may call for the offending player to leave the field for a set period of time, leaving their team with one less player. This makes it easier for the other team to find a way to score a goal.

THINK FAST!

DEFENDERS NEED TO BE ESPECIALLY CAREFUL NOT TO FOUL ATTACKERS IN THE CRITICAL SCORING AREA, WHICH IS 15 METERS (49 FEET) IN FRONT OF AND TO EACH SIDE OF THE GOAL AND 9 METERS (29.5 FEET) BEHIND THE GOAL.

Everyone needs to know how to shoot, but passing is often more important in lacrosse. Good passes make good goals.

The attacking players called second home and first home have scoring positions. A second home plays a bit farther from the goal than first home. Second home practices shooting from every angle and distance. Second home often runs the offense in women's lacrosse, like a point guard does in basketball. They tell attackers what plays to run or where to go to set up a scoring chance.

THINK FAST!

IF A FOUL IS THOUGHT TO BE KNOWINGLY DANGEROUS TO ANOTHER PLAYER, THE OFFENDING PLAYER MIGHT BE **DISQUALIFIED** FROM RETURNING TO THE GAME!

FREE POSITION

The penalty for some defensive fouls gives the offensive player a free position. This means other players must move away from the player with the ball. When the whistle restarts play, the player can run, pass, or shoot the ball at the net. It's a bit like a penalty kick in soccer.

The first home's job is to get shots off and score goals. They must be fast and able to slip away from defenders. First homes are the most offensive-minded players on the field.

First and second homes score the most goals in women's lacrosse, but anyone can put the ball in the net!

TIME TO TRY

Now that you know some basics of men's and women's lacrosse, think about trying it for yourself if you haven't. You'll find much more to learn about this historic game. While you can learn by watching, learning by playing is even more effective. Plus, a team is usually backed by a coach who can explain **strategy**.

While getting good at your position is important, figuring out how to play with others is even more essential for getting the ball by the goalie and into the net. Practice passing as much as scoring, and you'll be on your way to becoming an awesome lacrosse player!

LISTEN UP!

Coaches are a key part of every team. Especially when you're a beginner at a sport, coaches help you figure out what position may be best for your skills and teach you more about that role. Always listen to your coach, who can teach you how to play smart and—most important—play safe!

THINK FAST!

YOUTH LACROSSE LEAGUES HAVE THEIR OWN RULES. FOR EXAMPLE, BODY CHECKS USUALLY AREN'T ALLOWED.

Practice is where good teams become great. It can be fun to work on your skills!

GLOSSARY

accuracy: Being free of mistakes. Also, being able to hit the target.

agility: The ability to move around quickly and easily.

body check: To block an opponent in a game using the body.

disqualify: To stop or prevent someone from being a part of something, usually for having broken a rule.

intercept: To take control of a pass that was meant for a player on the other team.

maneuver: To move skillfully around.

NCAA: National Collegiate Athletic Association, the organization that controls college sports.

offside: Describing a team with more players over a certain line than is allowed by the rules.

penalty: Loss or harm caused because of a broken rule.

reflex: A fast reaction done without thinking.

strategy: A plan of action to achieve a goal.

FOR MORE INFORMATION

BOOKS

Marquardt, Meg. *Women in Lacrosse.* Lake Elmo, MN: Focus Readers, 2020.

Small, Cathleen. *Lacrosse.* New York, NY: Gareth Stevens Publishing LLP, 2019.

Wells, Donald. *Lacrosse.* New York, NY: AV2 by Weigl, 2020.

WEBSITES

Lacrosse Rules
www.ducksters.com/sports/lacrosserules.php
Read the basics of men's lacrosse here.

Rules of Women's Lacrosse
www.realbuzz.com/articles-interests/sports-activities/article/rules-of-womens-lacrosse/
Review the rules of women's lacrosse before you hit the field!

INDEX